The Ou

Other

The Owl and the Pussy Cat
and
Other Nonsense Poetry
by

Edward Lear

ALMA CLASSICS

ALMA CLASSICS
an imprint of

ALMA BOOKS LTD
3 Castle Yard
Richmond
Surrey TW10 6TF
United Kingdom
www.almaclassics.com

'Nonsense Songs' first published in *Nonsense Songs, Stories, Botany, and Alphabets* in 1871; 'More Nonsense' first published in *More Nonsense Pictures, Rhymes, Botany, etc* in 1872; additions and an amended 'Introduction' published in *More Nonsense* in 1888.
This edition first published by Alma Classics in 2019

Printed in Great Britain by CPI Group (UK) Ltd, Croydon CR0 4YY

ISBN: 978-1-84749-822-9

Contents

The Owl and the Pussy Cat
and
Other Nonsense Poetry

NONSENSE SONGS

The Owl and the Pussy Cat

I

The Owl and the Pussy Cat went to sea
    In a beautiful pea-green boat:
They took some honey, and plenty of money,
    Wrapped up in a five-pound note.
The Owl looked up to the stars above
    And sang to a small guitar,
"O lovely Pussy, O Pussy, my love,
    What a beautiful Pussy you are,
            You are,
            You are!
    What a beautiful Pussy you are!"

II

Pussy said to the Owl, "You elegant fowl,
    How charmingly sweet you sing!
Oh, let us be married! Too long we have tarried –
    But what shall we do for a ring?"
They sailed away, for a year and a day,
    To the land where the bong tree grows;
And there in a wood a Piggy-wig stood,
    With a ring at the end of his nose,
        His nose,
        His nose,
    With a ring at the end of his nose.

III

"Dear Pig, are you willing to sell for one shilling
    Your ring?" Said the Piggy, "I will."
So they took it away, and were married next day
    By the Turkey who lives on the hill.
They dinèd on mince and slices of quince,
    Which they ate with a runcible spoon,
And hand in hand, on the edge of the sand,
    They danced by the light of the moon,
        The moon,
        The moon,
    They danced by the light of the moon.

The Duck and the Kangaroo

I

Said the Duck to the Kangaroo,
  "Good gracious, how you hop,
Over the fields and the water too,
  As if you never would stop!
My life is a bore in this nasty pond,
And I long to go out in the world beyond:
  I wish I could hop like you,"
  Said the Duck to the Kangaroo.

II

"Please give me a ride on your back,"
    Said the Duck to the Kangaroo:
"I would sit quite still and say nothing but 'Quack'
    The whole of the long day through –
And we'd go the Dee, and the Jelly Bo Lee,
Over the land, and over the sea:
    Please take me a ride! Oh, do!"
    Said the Duck to the Kangaroo.

III

Said the Kangaroo to the Duck,
    "This requires some little reflection.
Perhaps, on the whole, it might bring me luck,
    And there seems but one objection –
Which is, if you'll let me speak so bold,
Your feet are unpleasantly wet and cold,
    And would probably give me the roo-
    Matiz," said the Kangaroo.

IV

Said the Duck, "As I sat on the rocks,
    I have thought over that completely,
And I bought four pairs of worsted socks,
    Which fit my web feet neatly;
And to keep out the cold I've bought a cloak,
And every day a cigar I'll smoke –
    All to follow my own dear true
    Love of a Kangaroo!"

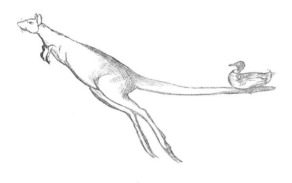

V

Said the Kangaroo, "I'm ready!
  All in the moonlight pale –
But to balance me well, dear Duck, sit steady,
  And quite at the end of my tail!"
So away they went with a hop and a bound,
And they hopped the whole world three times round.
  And who so happy – oh, who,
  As the Duck and the Kangaroo?

The Daddy-Long-Legs and the Fly

I

Once Mr Daddy-Long-Legs,
    Dressed in brown and grey,
Walked about upon the sands
    Upon a summer's day –
And there among the pebbles,
    When the wind was rather cold,
He met with Mr Floppy Fly,
    All dressed in blue and gold;
And as it was too soon to dine,
They drank some periwinkle wine,
And played an hour or two, or more,
At battlecock and shuttledore.

II

Said Mr Daddy-Long-Legs
    To Mr Floppy Fly,
"Why do you never come to court?
    I wish you'd tell me why.
All gold and shine, in dress so fine,
    You'd quite delight the court.
Why do you never go at all?
    I really think you *ought*!
And if you went, you'd see such sights!
Such rugs and jugs and candlelights!
And, more than all, the king and queen –
One in red, and one in green."

III

"Oh, Mr Daddy-Long-Legs,"
    Said Mr Floppy Fly,
"It's true I never go to court –
    And I will tell you why.
If I had six long legs like yours,

At once I'd go to court!
But, oh! I can't, because *my* legs
   Are so extremely short.
And I'm afraid the king and queen
(One in red, and one in green)
Would say aloud, 'You are not fit,
You Fly, to come to court a bit!'"

IV

"Oh, Mr Daddy-Long-Legs,"
   Said Mr Floppy Fly,
"I wish you'd sing one little song,
   One mumbian melody!
You used to sing so awful well
   In former days gone by;
But now you never sing at all –
   I wish you'd tell me why.
For if you would, the silvery sound
Would please the shrimps and cockles round,
And all the crabs would gladly come
To hear you sing, 'Ah, Hum di Hum!'"

V

Said Mr Daddy-Long-Legs,
    "I can never sing again;
And if you wish, I'll tell you why,
    Although it gives me pain.
For years I cannot hum a bit,
    Or sing the smallest song;
And this the dreadful reason is,
    My legs are grown too long!
My six long legs, all here and there,
Oppress my bosom with despair;
And if I stand or lie or sit,
I cannot sing one single bit!"

VI

So Mr Daddy-Long-Legs
    And Mr Floppy Fly
Sat down in silence by the sea
    And gazed upon the sky.
They said, "This is a dreadful thing!
    The world has all gone wrong,

Since one has legs too short by half,
    The other much too long!
One never more can go to court,
Because his legs have grown too short;
The other cannot sing a song,
Because his legs have grown too long!"

VII

Then Mr Daddy-Long-Legs
    And Mr Floppy Fly
Rushed downward to the foamy sea
    With one sponge-taneous cry –

And there they found a little boat,
    Whose sails were pink and grey;
And off they sailed among the waves,
    Far and far away.
They sailed across the silent main,
And reached the great Gromboolian Plain;
And there they play for evermore
At battlecock and shuttledore.

The Jumblies

I

They went to sea in a sieve, they did –
  In a sieve they went to sea:
In spite of all their friends could say,
On a winter's morn, on a stormy day,
  In a sieve they went to sea!
And when the sieve turned round and round,
And every one cried "You'll all be drowned!"
They called aloud, "Our sieve ain't big,

But we don't care a button, we don't care a fig!
  In a sieve we'll go to sea!"
    Far and few, far and few,
      Are the lands where the Jumblies live;
      Their heads are green, and their hands are blue,
      And they went to sea in a sieve.

II

They sailed away in a sieve, they did –
  In a sieve they sailed so fast,
With only a beautiful pea-green veil
Tied with a ribbon, by way of a sail,
  To a small tobacco-pipe mast.
And everyone said who saw them go,
"Oh, won't they be soon upset, you know!
For the sky is dark, and the voyage is long –
And happen what may, it's extremely wrong
  In a sieve to sail so fast!"
    Far and few, far and few,
      Are the lands where the Jumblies live;
      Their heads are green, and their hands are blue,
      And they went to sea in a sieve.

III

The water it soon came in, it did –
  The water it soon came in:
So to keep them dry, they wrapped their feet
In a pinky paper all folded neat,
  And they fastened it down with a pin.
And they passed the night in a crockery jar,
And each of them said, "How wise we are!
Though the sky be dark, and the voyage be long,
Yet we never can think we were rash or wrong,
  While round in our sieve we spin!"
    Far and few, far and few,
      Are the lands where the Jumblies live;
      Their heads are green, and their hands are blue,
        And they went to sea in a sieve.

IV

And all night long they sailed away –
  And when the sun went down,
They whistled and warbled a moony song

To the echoing sound of a coppery gong,
    In the shade of the mountains brown.
"O, Timballoo! How happy we are,
When we live in a sieve and a crockery jar!
And all night long in the moonlight pale,
We sail away with a pea-green sail
    In the shade of the mountains brown."
        Far and few, far and few,
            Are the lands where the Jumblies live;
            Their heads are green, and their hands are blue,
                And they went to sea in a sieve.

V

They sailed to the Western Sea, they did –
    To a land all covered with trees:
And they bought an owl, and a useful cart,
And a pound of rice, and a cranberry tart,
    And a hive of silvery bees;
And they bought a pig, and some green jackdaws,
And a lovely monkey with lollipop paws,
And forty bottles of ring-bo-ree,
    And no end of Stilton cheese.

Far and few, far and few,
 Are the lands where the Jumblies live;
Their heads are green, and their hands are blue,
 And they went to sea in a sieve.

VI

And in twenty years they all came back –
 In twenty years or more;
And every one said, "How tall they've grown!
For they've been to the Lakes, and the Terrible Zone,
 And the hills of the Chankly Bore."
And they drank their health, and gave them a feast
Of dumplings made of beautiful yeast;
And every one said, "If we only live,
We too will go to sea in a sieve,
 To the hills of the Chankly Bore."
  Far and few, far and few,
   Are the lands where the Jumblies live;
   Their heads are green, and their hands are blue,
    And they went to sea in a sieve.

The Nutcrackers and the
Sugar-Tongs

I

The Nutcrackers sat by a plate on the table,
   The Sugar-Tongs sat by a plate at his side,
And the Nutcrackers said, "Don't you wish we
      were able
    Along the blue hills and green meadows to ride?
Must we drag on this stupid existence for ever,
   So idle and weary, so full of remorse,
While everyone else takes his pleasure, and never
   Seems happy unless he is riding a horse?

II

"Don't you think we could ride without being
    instructed,
   Without any saddle or bridle or spur?
Our legs are so long, and so aptly constructed,
   I'm sure that an accident could not occur.
Let us all of a sudden hop down from the table,
   And hustle downstairs, and each jump on a
      horse!
Shall we try? Shall we go? Do you think we are
      able?"
   The Sugar-Tongs answered distinctly, "Of
      course!"

III

So down the long staircase they hopped in a
      minute;
   The Sugar-Tongs snapped, and the Crackers
      said, "Crack!"
The stable was open; the horses were in it:
   Each took out a pony and jumped on his back.

The Cat in a fright scrambled out of the doorway;
  The Mice tumbled out of a bundle of hay;
The brown and white Rats, and the black ones
    from Norway,
    Screamed out, "They are taking the horses
    away!"

IV

The whole of the household was filled with
    amazement:
  The Cups and the Saucers danced madly about;
The Plates and the Dishes looked out of the
    casement;
  The Salt Cellar stood on his head with a shout;
The Spoons, with a clatter, looked out of the
    lattice;
  The Mustard Pot climbed up the gooseberry pies;
The Soup-Ladle peeped through a heap of veal
    patties
  And squeaked with a ladle-like scream of
    surprise.

V

The Frying Pan said, "It's an awful delusion!"
    The Tea Kettle hissed and grew black in the
        face;
And they all rushed downstairs in the wildest
      confusion
    To see the great Nutcracker-Sugar-Tong race.
And out of the stable, with screamings and
      laughter
    (Their ponies were cream-coloured, speckled
      with brown),
The Nutcrackers first, and the Sugar-Tongs after,
    Rode all round the yard, and then all round the
      town.

VI

They rode through the street, and they rode by
      the station;
    They galloped away to the beautiful shore;
In silence they rode, and "made no observation"
    Save this: "We will never go back any more!"

And still you might hear, till they rode out of
     hearing,
    The Sugar-Tongs snap and the Crackers say
     "Crack!" –
Till far in the distance their forms disappearing,
    They faded away, and they never came back!

Calico Pie

I

Calico pie,
  The little Birds fly
Down to the calico tree;
  Their wings were blue,
  And they sang "Tilly-loo!"
  Till away they flew –
And they never came back to me!
  They never came back,
  They never came back,
They never came back to me!

II

Calico jam,
The little Fish swam
Over the Syllabub Sea.
He took off his hat
To the Sole and the Sprat,
And the Willeby-wat –

But he never came back to me!
He never came back,
He never came back,
He never came back to me!

III

Calico ban,
  The little Mice ran,
To be ready in time for tea;
  Flippity flup,
  They drank it all up,
  And danced in the cup –
But they never came back to me!
  They never came back,
  They never came back,
They never came back to me!

IV

Calico drum,
  The Grasshoppers come,
The Butterfly, Beetle and Bee,

Over the ground,
Around and round,
With a hop and a bound –

But they never came back!
They never came back,
They never came back,
They never came back to me!

Mr and Mrs Spikky Sparrow

I

On a little piece of wood
Mr Spikky Sparrow stood;
Mrs Sparrow sat close by,
A-making of an insect pie
For her little children five,
In the nest and all alive –
Singing with a cheerful smile
To amuse them all the while,
    "Twikky wikky wikky wee,
    Wikky bikky twikky tee,
        Spikky bikky bee!"

II

Mrs Spikky Sparrow said,
"Spikky, darling! In my head
Many thoughts of trouble come,
Like to flies upon a plum!
All last night, among the trees,
I heard you cough, I heard you sneeze;
And thought I, 'It's come to that
Because he does not wear a hat!'
    Chippy wippy sikky tee,
    Bikky wikky tikky mee,
      Spikky chippy wee!

III

"Not that you are growing old –
But the nights are growing cold.
No one stays out all night long
Without a hat: I'm sure it's wrong!"
Mr Spikky said, "How kind,
Dear, you are, to speak your mind!

All your life I wish you luck!
You are, you are, a lovely duck!
    Witchy witchy witchy wee,
    Twitchy witchy witchy bee,
      Tikky tikky tee!

IV

"I was also sad, and thinking,
When one day I saw you winking,
And I heard you sniffle-snuffle,
And I saw your feathers ruffle:
To myself I sadly said,
'She's neuralgia in her head!
That dear head has nothing on it!
Ought she not to wear a bonnet?'
    Witchy kitchy kitchy wee,
    Spikky wikky mikky bee,
      Chippy wippy chee!

V

"Let us both fly up to town:
There I'll buy you such a gown!

Which, completely in the fashion,
You shall tie a sky-blue sash on;
And a pair of slippers neat
To fit your darling little feet,
So that you will look and feel
Quite galloobious and genteel.
   Jikky wikky bikky see,
   Chicky bikky wikky bee,
     Twicky witchy wee!"

VI

So they both to London went,
Alighting on the Monument;
Whence they flew down swiftly – pop! –
Into Moses' wholesale shop:
There they bought a hat and bonnet,
And a gown with spots upon it,
A satin sash of Cloxam blue,
And a pair of slippers too.
   Zikky wikky mikky bee,
   Witchy witchy mitchy kee,
     Sikky tikky wee!

VII

Then, when so completely dressed,
Back they flew, and reached their nest.
Their children cried, "O Ma and Pa!
How truly beautiful you are!"
Said they, "We trust that cold or pain
We shall never feel again –
While, perched on tree or house or steeple,
We now shall look like other people.

Witchy witchy witchy wee,
Twikky mikky bikky bee,
Zikky sikky tee!"

The Broom, the Shovel, the Poker
and the Tongs

I

The Broom and the Shovel, the Poker and Tongs,
    They all took a drive in the park;
And they each sang a song – ding-a-dong, ding-
    a-dong! –
    Before they went back in the dark.
Mr Poker, he sat quite upright in the coach;
    Mr Tongs made a clatter and clash;
Miss Shovel was dressed all in black (with a brooch);
    Mrs Broom was in blue (with a sash).
        Ding-a-dong, ding-a-dong!
        And they all sang a song!

II

"O Shovely so lovely!" the Poker he sang,
   "You have perfectly conquered my heart.
Ding-a-dong, ding-a-dong! If you're pleased with
     my song,
   I will feed you with cold apple tart.
When you scrape up the coals with a delicate sound,
   You enrapture my life with delight!
Your nose is so shiny, your head is so round,
   And your shape is so slender and bright!
     Ding-a-dong, ding-a-dong!
     Ain't you pleased with my song?"

III

"Alas! Mrs Broom," sighed the Tongs in his song,
   "Oh, is it because I'm so thin,
And my legs are so long – ding-a-dong, ding-a-dong! –
   That you don't care about me a pin?
Ah, fairest of creatures, when sweeping the room,
   Ah, why don't you heed my complaint?
Must you needs be so cruel, you beautiful Broom,

Because you are covered with paint?
    Ding-a-dong, ding-a-dong!
    You are certainly wrong!"

IV

Mrs Broom and Miss Shovel together they sang,
    "What nonsense you're singing today!"
Said the Shovel, "I'll certainly hit you a bang!"
    Said the Broom, "And I'll sweep you away!"
So the Coachman drove homeward as fast as he could,
    Perceiving their anger with pain;
But they put on the kettle, and little by little
    They all became happy again.
        Ding-a-dong, ding-a-dong!
        There's an end of my song!

— 40 —

The Table and
the Chair

I

Said the Table to the Chair,
"You can hardly be aware
How I suffer from the heat
And from chilblains on my feet!
If we took a little walk,
We might have a little talk;
Pray let us take the air,"
Said the Table to the Chair.

II

Said the Chair unto the Table,
"Now, you *know* we are not able!
How foolishly you talk,
When you know we *cannot* walk!"
Said the Table with a sigh,
"It can do no harm to try.
I've as many legs as you:
Why can't we walk on two?"

III

So they both went slowly down
And walked about the town
With a cheerful bumpy sound
As they toddled round and round –
And everybody cried,
As they hastened to their side,
"See, the Table and the Chair
Have come out to take the air!"

IV

But in going down an alley,
To a castle in a valley,
They completely lost their way
And wandered all the day –
Till, to see them safely back,
They paid a Ducky-Quack,
And a Beetle and a Mouse,
Who took them to their house.

V

Then they whispered to each other,
"O delightful little brother,
What a lovely walk we've taken!
Let us dine on beans and bacon."
So the Ducky and the leetle
Browny-Mousy and the Beetle
Dined, and danced upon their heads
Till they toddled to their beds.

MORE NONSENSE

Introduction

N OFFERING THIS little book to the public, I am glad to take the opportunity of recording the pleasure I have received at the appreciation its predecessor has met with, as attested by its wide circulation, and by the universally kind notices of it from the press. To have been the means of administering innocent mirth to thousands may surely be a just motive for satisfaction, and an excuse for grateful expression.

At the same time, I am desirous of adding a few words as to the history of the previously published volume, viz. the first or original *Book of Nonsense*, relating to which many absurd reports have crept into circulation, such as that it was the composition of the late Lord Brougham, the late Earl of Derby, etc. – that the rhymes and pictures are by different persons, or that the whole have a symbolical meaning, etc., etc. – whereas every one of the rhymes was composed by myself, and every one of the illustrations drawn by my own hand at the time the verses were made. Moreover, in no portion of these Nonsense drawings have I ever allowed any caricature of private or public persons to appear, and throughout, more care than might be supposed has been given to make the subjects incapable of misinterpretation – "Nonsense", pure and absolute, having been my aim throughout.

As for the persistently absurd report of the late Earl of Derby being the author of the first *Book of Nonsense*, I may relate an incident which occurred to me four summers ago, the first that gave me any insight into the origin of the rumour.

I was on my way from London to Guildford, in a railway carriage containing, besides myself, one passenger, an elderly gentleman. Presently, however, two ladies entered, accompanied by two little boys. These, who had just had a copy of the *Book of Nonsense* given them, were loud in their delight, and by degrees infected the whole party with their mirth.

"How grateful," said the old gentleman to the two ladies, "all children and parents too ought to be to the statesman who has given his time to composing that charming book!"

(The ladies looked puzzled, as indeed was I, the author.)

"Do you not know who is the writer of it?" asked the gentleman.

"The name is 'Edward Lear'," said one of the ladies.

"Ah!" said the first speaker. "So it is printed – but that is only a whim of the real author, the Earl of Derby. 'Edward' is his Christian name – and, as you may see, LEAR is only EARL transposed."

"But," said the lady doubtingly, "here is a dedication to the great-grandchildren, grand-nephews and grand-nieces of Edward, thir-teenth Earl of Derby, by the author, Edward Lear."

"That," replied the other, "is simply a piece of mystification; I am in a position to know that the whole book was composed and illustrated by Lord Derby himself. In fact, there is no such a person at all as Edward Lear."

"Yet," said the other lady, "some friends of mine tell me they know Mr Lear."

"Quite a mistake! Completely a mistake!" said the old gentleman, becoming rather angry at the contradiction. "I am well aware of what I am saying. I can inform you, no such a person as 'Edward Lear' exists!"

Hitherto I had kept silence, but as my hat was – as well as my handkerchief and stick – largely marked inside with my name, and as I happened to have in my pocket several letters addressed to me, the temptation was too great to resist: so, flashing all these articles at once on my would-be extinguisher's attention, I speedily reduced him to silence.

Long years ago, in days when much of my time was passed in a country house where children and mirth abounded, the lines beginning "There was an old man of Tobago" were suggested to me by a valued friend as a form of verse lending itself to limitless variety for rhymes and pictures – and thenceforth the greater part of the original drawings and verses for the first *Book of Nonsense* were struck off with a pen, no assistance ever having been given me in any way but that of uproarious delight and welcome at the appearance of every new absurdity.

Most of these drawings and rhymes were reproduced and issued in the original *Book of Nonsense.* But many editions of that work having been exhausted, and the call for it still continuing, I added a considerable number of subjects to those previously published, and these form the present volume.

EDWARD LEAR
Villa Emily, San Remo

There was a young person of Bantry,
Who frequently slept in the pantry;
   When disturbed by the mice,
   She appeased them with rice,
That judicious young person of Bantry.

There was an old man at a junction,
Whose feelings were wrung with compunction;
   When they said "The Train's gone!"
   He exclaimed, "How forlorn!"
But remained on the rails of the junction.

There was an old man who when little
Fell casually into a kettle;
  But, growing too stout,
  He could never get out,
So he passed all his life in that kettle.

There was an old man whose despair
Induced him to purchase a hare:
 Whereon one fine day
 He rode wholly away,
Which partly assuaged his despair.

There was an old person of Minety,
Who purchased five hundred and ninety
    Large apples and pears,
    Which he threw unawares
At the heads of the people of Minety.

There was an old man of Thermopylae,
Who never did anything properly;
    But they said, "If you choose
    To boil eggs in your shoes,
You shall never remain in Thermopylae."

There was an old person of Deal,
Who in walking used only his heel;
 When they said "Tell us why?"
 He made no reply,
That mysterious old person of Deal.

There was an old man on the Humber,
Who dined on a cake of burnt umber;
   When he said "It's enough!"
    They only said, "Stuff!
You amazing old man on the Humber!"

There was an old man of Blackheath,
Whose head was adorned with a wreath
   Of lobsters and spice,
   Pickled onions and mice,
That uncommon old man of Blackheath.

There was an old man of Toulouse,
Who purchased a new pair of shoes;
     When they asked "Are they pleasant?"
     He said, "Not at present!"
That turbid old man of Toulouse.

There was an old person in black:
A grasshopper jumped on his back;
   When it chirped in his ear,
   He was smitten with fear,
That helpless old person in black.

There was an old man in a barge,
Whose nose was exceedingly large;
    But in fishing by night,
    It supported a light,
Which helped that old man in a barge.

There was an old man of Dunrose;
A parrot seized hold of his nose.
  When he grew melancholy,
  They said, "His name's Polly,"
Which soothed that old man of Dunrose.

There was an old person of Bromley,
Whose ways were not cheerful or comely;
   He sat in the dust,
   Eating spiders and crust,
That unpleasing old person of Bromley.

There was an old man of Dunluce,
Who went out to sea on a goose;
   When he'd gone out a mile,
   He observed with a smile,
"It is time to return to Dunluce."

There was an old person of Pinner,
As thin as a lath, if not thinner;
    They dressed him in white,
    And rolled him up tight,
That elastic old person of Pinner.

There was an old man in a marsh,
Whose manners were futile and harsh;
   He sat on a log
   And sang songs to a frog,
That instructive old man in a marsh.

There was an old man of Deeside,
Whose hat was exceedingly wide;
    But he said, "Do not fail,
    If it happen to hail,
To come under my hat at Deeside!"

There was an old person of Bree,
Who frequented the depths of the sea;
   She nursed the small fishes,
   And washed all the dishes,
And swam back again into Bree.

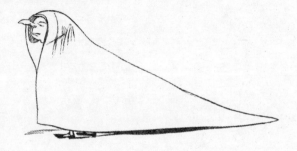

There was a young person in green,
Who seldom was fit to be seen;
    She wore a long shawl
    Over bonnet and all,
Which enveloped that person in green.

There was an old person of Wick,
Who said, "Tick-a-Tick, Tick-a-Tick;
  Chickabee, Chickabaw."
    And he said nothing more,
That laconic old person of Wick.

There was an old man at a station,
Who made a promiscuous oration;
   But they said, "Take some snuff!
   You have talked quite enough,
You afflicting old man at a station!"

There was an old man of Three Bridges,
Whose mind was distracted by midges;
    He sat on a wheel
    Eating underdone veal,
Which relieved that old man of Three Bridges.

There was an old person of Fife,
Who was greatly disgusted with life;
    They sang him a ballad
    And fed him on salad,
Which cured that old person of Fife.

There was an old person of Shields,
Who frequented the valleys and fields;
  All the mice and the cats,
  And the snakes and the rats,
Followed after that person of Shields.

There was an old person of China,
Whose daughters were Jiska and Dinah,
  Amelia and Fluffy,
  Olivia and Chuffy,
And all of them settled in China.

There was an old man of the Dargle,
Who purchased six barrels of gargle;
   For he said, "I'll sit still,
   And will roll them downhill,
For the fish in the depths of the Dargle."

There was an old man who screamed out
Whenever they knocked him about;
  So they took off his boots,
  And fed him with fruits,
And continued to knock him about.

There was an old person of Brill,
Who purchased a shirt with a frill;
    But they said, "Don't you wish
    You mayn't look like a fish,
You obsequious old person of Brill?"

There was an old person of Slough,
Who danced at the end of a bough;
  But they said, "If you sneeze,
  You might damage the trees,
You imprudent old person of Slough."

There was a young person in red,
Who carefully covered her head
    With a bonnet of leather
    And three lines of feather,
Besides some long ribbons of red.

There was a young person in pink,
Who called out for something to drink;
   But they said, "O my daughter,
    There's nothing but water!" –
Which vexed that young person in pink.

There was a young lady in white,
Who looked out at the depths of the night;
   But the birds of the air
   Filled her heart with despair
And oppressed that young lady in white.

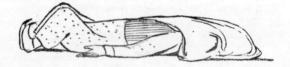

There was an old man of Hong Kong,
Who never did anything wrong;
   He lay on his back,
   With his head in a sack,
That innocuous old man of Hong Kong.

There was an old person of Putney,
Whose food was roast spiders and chutney,
  Which he took with his tea,
  Within sight of the sea,
That romantic old person of Putney.

There was an old person of Woking,
Whose mind was perverse and provoking;
   He sat on a rail
   With his head in a pail,
That illusive old person of Woking.

There was an old lady of France,
Who taught little ducklings to dance;
  When she said "Tick-a-tack!"
  They only said, "Quack!" –
Which grieved that old lady of France.

There was a young lady in blue,
Who said, "Is it you? Is it you?"
　　When they said "Yes, it is",
　　She replied only, "Whizz!" –
That ungracious young lady in blue.

There was an old man in a garden,
Who always begged everyone's pardon;
When they asked him "What for?"
He replied, "You're a bore!
And I trust you'll go out of my garden."

There was an old person of Loo,
Who said, "What on earth shall I do?"
    When they said "Go away!"
    She continued to stay,
That vexatious old person of Loo.

There was an old person of Pisa,
Whose daughters did nothing to please her;
   She dressed them in grey
   And banged them all day
Round the walls of the city of Pisa.

There was an old person of Florence,
Who held mutton chops in abhorrence;
   He purchased a bustard
   And fried him in mustard,
Which choked that old person of Florence.

There was an old person of Sheen,
Whose expression was calm and serene;
    He sat in the water
    And drank bottled porter,
That placid old person of Sheen.

There was an old person of Ware,
Who rode on the back of a bear;
   When they asked "Does it trot?"
   He said, "Certainly not!
He's a Moppsikon Floppsikon bear!"

There was an old person of Dean,
Who dined on one pea and one bean;
    For he said, "More than that,
    Would make me too fat" –
That cautious old person of Dean.

There was a young person of Janina,
Whose uncle was always a-fanning her;
    When he fanned off her head,
    She smiled sweetly and said,
"You propitious old person of Janina!"

There was an old person of Down,
Whose face was adorned with a frown;
When he opened the door,
For one minute or more,
He alarmed all the people of Down.

There was an old person of Cassel,
Whose nose finished off in a tassel;
  But they called out, "Oh well!
  Don't it look like a bell!" –
Which perplexed that old person of Cassel.

There was an old man of Kashmir,
Whose movements were scroobious and queer;
    Being slender and tall,
    He looked over a wall
And perceived two fat ducks of Kashmir.

There was an old person of Hove,
Who frequented the depths of a grove,
  Where he studied his books
  With the wrens and the rooks,
That tranquil old person of Hove.

There was an old man of Spithead,
Who opened the window and said,
    "Fil-jomble, fil-jumble,
    Fil-rumble-come-tumble!" –
That doubtful old man of Spithead.

There was an old man on the border,
Who lived in the utmost disorder;
   He danced with the cat
   And made tea in his hat –
Which vexed all the folks on the border.

There was an old man of Dundalk,
Who tried to teach fishes to walk;
   When they tumbled down dead,
   He grew weary and said,
"I had better go back to Dundalk!"

There was an old man of Dumbree,
Who taught little owls to drink tea;
　　For he said, "To eat mice
　　Is not proper or nice" –
That amiable man of Dumbree.

There was an old person of Jodd,
Whose ways were perplexing and odd;
   She purchased a whistle,
   And sat on a thistle,
And squeaked to the people of Jodd.

There was an old person of Shoreham,
Whose habits were marked by decorum;
   He bought an umbrella
   And sat in the cellar –
Which pleased all the people of Shoreham.

There was an old man whose remorse
Induced him to drink caper sauce;
    For they said, "If mixed up
    With some cold claret cup,
It will certainly soothe your remorse!"

There was an old person of Wilts,
Who constantly walked upon stilts;
   He wreathed them with lilies
   And daffy-down-dillies,
That elegant person of Wilts.

There was an old person of Pett,
Who was partly consumed by regret;
    He sat in a cart
    And ate cold apple tart,
Which relieved that old person of Pett.

There was an old man of Port Grigor,
Whose actions were noted for vigour;
   He stood on his head
    Till his waistcoat turned red,
That eclectic old man of Port Grigor.

There was an old person of Bar,
Who passed all her life in a jar,
  Which she painted pea-green
  To appear more serene,
That placid old person of Bar.

There was an old man of West Dumpet,
Who possessed a large nose like a trumpet;
    When he blew it aloud,
    It astonished the crowd,
And was heard through the whole of West Dumpet.

There was an old person of Grange,
Whose manners were scroobious and strange;
   He sailed to St Blubb
   In a waterproof tub,
That aquatic old person of Grange.

There was an old person of Nice,
Whose associates were usually geese;
   They walked out together
   In all sorts of weather –
That affable person of Nice!

There was a young person of Kew,
Whose virtues and vices were few;
   But with blamable haste
   She devoured some hot paste,
Which destroyed that young person of Kew.

There was an old person of Sark,
Who made an unpleasant remark;
    But they said, "Don't you see
    What a brute you must be,
You obnoxious old person of Sark!"

There was an old person of Filey,
Of whom his acquaintance spoke highly;
   He danced perfectly well,
    To the sound of a bell,
And delighted the people of Filey.

There was an old man of El Hums,
Who lived upon nothing but crumbs,
   Which he picked off the ground,
   With the other birds round,
In the roads and the lanes of El Hums.

There was an old man of Dunblane,
Who greatly resembled a crane;
  But they said, "Is it wrong,
  Since your legs are so long,
To request you won't stay in Dunblane?"

There was an old person of Hyde,
Who walked by the shore with his bride,
    Till a crab who came near
    Filled their bosoms with fear,
And they said, "Would we'd never left Hyde!"

There was an old person of Rimini,
Who said, "Gracious! Goodness! Oh Gimini!"
   When they said "Please be still!"
   She ran down a hill,
And was never more heard of at Rimini.

There was an old person of Cannes,
Who purchased three fowls and a fan;
    Those she placed on a stool,
    And to make them feel cool
She constantly fanned them at Cannes.

There was an old person of Bude,
Whose deportment was vicious and crude;
   He wore a large ruff
   Of pale straw-coloured stuff,
Which perplexed all the people of Bude.

There was an old person of Ickley,
Who could not abide to ride quickly;
   He rode to Karnak
   On a tortoise's back,
That moony old person of Ickley.

There was an old man of Ancona,
Who found a small dog with no owner,
   Which he took up and down
   All the streets of the town –
That anxious old man of Ancona.

There was an old person of Barnes,
Whose garments were covered with darns;
　　But they said, "Without doubt,
　　You will soon wear them out,
You luminous person of Barnes!"

There was an old person of Blythe,
Who cut up his meat with a scythe;
    When they said "Well! I never!"
    He cried, "Scythes for ever!" –
That lively old person of Blythe.

There was an old person of Ealing,
Who was wholly devoid of good feeling;
   He drove a small gig,
   With three owls and a pig,
Which distressed all the people of Ealing.

There was an old person of Bray,
Who sang through the whole of the day
   To his ducks and his pigs,
   Whom he fed upon figs,
That valuable person of Bray.

There was an old person of Bow,
Whom nobody happened to know;
    So they gave him some soap,
    And said coldly, "We hope
You will go back directly to Bow!"

There was an old person in grey,
Whose feelings were tinged with dismay;
   She purchased two parrots
   And fed them with carrots,
Which pleased that old person in grey.

There was an old person of Crowle,
Who lived in the nest of an owl;
    When they screamed in the nest,
    He screamed out with the rest,
That depressing old person of Crowle.

There was an old person of Brigg,
Who purchased no end of a wig;
   So that only his nose
   And the end of his toes
Could be seen when he walked about Brigg.

There was a young lady of Greenwich,
Whose garments were bordered with spinach;
   But a large spotty calf
   Bit her shawl quite in half,
Which alarmed that young lady of Greenwich.

There was an old person of Rye,
Who went up to town on a fly;
   But they said, "If you cough,
   You are safe to fall off,
You abstemious old person of Rye!"

There was an old man of Messina,
Whose daughter was named Opsibeena;
    She wore a small wig
    And rode out on a pig,
To the perfect delight of Messina.

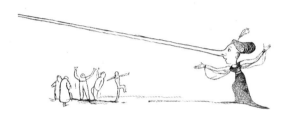

There is a young lady, whose nose
Continually prospers and grows;
    When it grew out of sight,
    She exclaimed in a fright,
"Oh, farewell to the end of my nose!"

There was an old person of Sestri,
Who sat himself down in the vestry;
    When they said "You are wrong!"
    He merely said "Bong!" –
That repulsive old person of Sestri.

There was an old man in a tree,
Whose whiskers were lovely to see;
    But the birds of the air
    Plucked them perfectly bare,
To make themselves nests in that tree.

There was a young lady of Corsica,
Who purchased a little brown saucy cur,
   Which she fed upon ham
   And hot raspberry jam,
That expensive young lady of Corsica.

There was a young lady of Firle,
Whose hair was addicted to curl;
   It curled up a tree
   And all over the sea,
That expansive young lady of Firle.

There was an old lady of Winchelsea,
Who said, "If you needle or pin shall see
    On the floor of my room,
    Sweep it up with the broom!" –
That exhaustive old Lady of Winchelsea!

There was a young person whose history
Was always considered a mystery;
   She sat in a ditch,
   Although no one knew which,
And composed a small treatise on history.

There was an old man of Boulak,
Who sat on a crocodile's back;
    But they said, "Tow'rds the night
    He may probably bite,
Which might vex you, old man of Boulak!"

There was an old man of Ibreem,
Who suddenly threatened to scream;
    But they said, "If you do,
    We will thump you quite blue,
You disgusting old man of Ibreem!"

There was an old person of Stroud,
Who was horribly jammed in a crowd;
  Some she slew with a kick,
  Some she scrunched with a stick,
That impulsive old person of Stroud.

There was an old man of Thames Ditton,
Who called out for something to sit on;
    But they brought him a hat
    And said, "Sit upon that,
You abruptious old man of Thames Ditton!"

There was an old person of Skye,
Who waltzed with a bluebottle fly;
    They buzzed a sweet tune
    To the light of the moon
And entranced all the people of Skye.

There was a young person of Ayr,
Whose head was remarkably square:
   On the top, in fine weather,
   She wore a gold feather –
Which dazzled the people of Ayr.

There was an old person of Newry,
Whose manners were tinctured with fury;
   He tore all the rugs
   And broke all the jugs
Within twenty miles' distance of Newry.

There was a young lady of Poole,
Whose soup was excessively cool;
　　So she put it to boil
　　By the side of some oil,
That ingenious young lady of Poole.

There was a young lady of Turkey,
Who wept when the weather was murky;
   When the day turned out fine,
   She ceased to repine,
That capricious young lady of Turkey.

There was an old man of Peru,
Who never knew what he should do;
  So he tore off his hair
  And behaved like a bear,
That intrinsic old man of Peru.

Biographical Note

Edward Lear was born in Upper Holloway, London, in 1812, the twentieth of twenty-one children. With financial difficulties plaguing his father, the young Edward was placed in the charge of his eldest sister, Ann, who was responsible for his upbringing. He attended school for a brief period, but he was mostly educated at home by Ann and another sister, Sarah. This lack of formal education may have been the result of continuous ill health, with Edward suffering from asthma, bronchitis and epilepsy. It was his sisters who instructed him in the art of drawing and painting, and from the age of fifteen, such work was to earn him his living.

By 1829 he had become an ornithological draughtsman, serving an apprenticeship of sorts under the famed Prideaux John Selby (1788–1867). Following the opening of the Zoological Gardens in London in 1829, Lear was granted permission to make drawings of the parrots.

This led to the publication in 1832 of Lear's *Illustrations of the Family of Psittacidæ, or Parrots*. Over the next few years he contributed to works by Selby and Sir William Jardine (1800–74), among others, forging a reputation as one of the country's foremost ornithological draughtsman. Lord Stanley, the 13th Earl of Derby, was one such admirer, and saw Lear as just the artist he needed to produce an accurate record of the menagerie he had been building at his home at Knowsley, near Liverpool. Between 1831 and 1837, Lear spent large periods of time at Knowsley, making drawings and watercolours of the birds and beasts that dwelt there.

The large country house, "where mirth and children abounded", as Lear later recalled, was also the setting for the drawing and penning of much of the material for *A Book of Nonsense*.

In 1837, with Lear's poor eyesight deteriorating further and the climate of northern England exacerbating his bronchitis and asthma, Lord Stanley offered to send Lear to Rome, in the hope that the climate would prove more congenial to his health.

Landscape work had by now taken the place of natural history for Lear. His travels around Italy produced *Views in Rome and its Environs* in 1841 and *Illustrated Excursions in Italy* in 1846. Queen Victoria was so impressed with the latter that she asked Lear to give her twelve drawing lessons. 1846 also saw the publication of *A Book of Nonsense*, a collection of nonsense verse and accompanying drawings. It was published to little fanfare, yet the revised third edition, published in 1861, proved an enormous success and swept what we now know as the limerick – the term is a late-nineteenth-century coinage – into the public consciousness. Twenty-four editions followed in Lear's lifetime alone, and the book has never been out of print.

Lear continued to live an itinerant artist's life, with years spent travelling through Greece and the Greek islands. It was in 1867, however, when the poet John Addington Symonds's daughter Janet was ill and confined to her bed, that Lear wrote for her 'The Owl and the Pussycat', which was later published in *Nonsense Songs, Stories, Botany and Alphabets* (1871) and became one of the most enduringly popular poems written in the English language.

Lear died of heart disease in 1888 at his villa in San Remo. Lear's achievements as a painter were overlooked for many years due to his enormous success as a writer of humorous verse. Throughout the twentieth century, however, this lopsided view began to be redressed, and he is now recognized as a skilled and powerful landscape painter, as well as a towering figure in ornithological drawing and the nation's favourite nonsense writer.

Publisher's Note

The first line of the poem on p. 105 has been amended to read "man" rather than the original "person" for reasons of prosody.

The Crocodile
Fyodor Dostoevsky

The Death of a Civil Servant
Anton Chekhov

The Decay of Lying
Oscar Wilde

The Dictionary of
Received Ideas
Gustave Flaubert

Directions to Servants
Jonathan Swift

Dirty Limericks
Anonymous